ROMAN PLACES

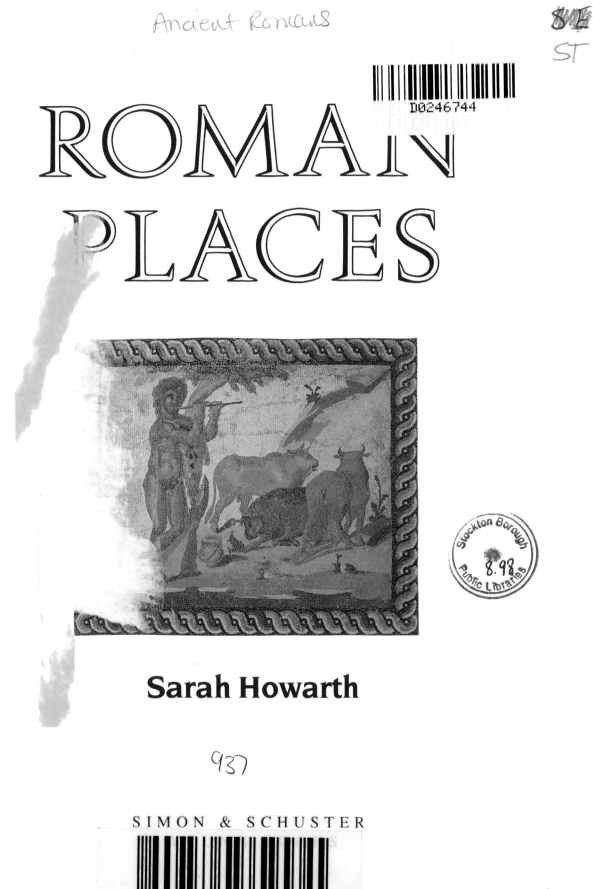

Sarah Howarth

SIMON & SCHUSTER

For the memory of Fr T. D. Healy

First published in Great Britain in 1993 by

Simon & Schuster Young Books
Campus 400
Maylands Avenue
Hemel Hempstead
Hertfordshire HP2 7EZ

Designed by Neil Adams
Illustrations by Philip McNeill

Text copyright © 1993 by Sarah Howarth
Illustrations copyright © 1993 by Philip McNeill

Typeset by DP Press Ltd, Sevenoaks, Kent

Printed and bound by Proost International Book Co., Belgium

A CIP record for this book can be obtained from the British Library

ISBN 0-7500-1308-7

Picture acknowledgements

Picture research by Donna Thynne

Front cover: The Bridgeman Art Library
Spine: Archiv für Kunst und Geschichte

Archiv für Kunst und Geschichte: contents page, p.9, p.15, p.20, p.28, p.32, p.35, p.44; British Museum: p.10; C.M. Dixon/Photo Resources: p.17; Werner Forman Archive: p.11, p.16, p.31; Sonia Halliday Photographs: frontispiece, p.8, p.23, p.30, p.38, p.45; Michael Holford Photographs: p.19, p.26, p.34; The Mansell Collection Ltd: p.12, p.13, p.21, p.24, p.25, p.36, p.40, p.41; Scala: p.7, p.14, p.18, p.22, p.27, p.29, p.33, p.42; Tullie House Museum, Carlisle: p.32, p.37, p.39

CONTENTS

INTRODUCTION

The city of Rome has a long history. It grew from a collection of huts on the hills above the River Tiber in Italy about 800 years before the birth of Christ (BC), into a city teeming with soldiers, traders, slaves, politicians, thinkers and thieves. Its armies conquered first the rest of the Italian peninsula, and then other lands.

Everywhere they went, the Romans made a great impact. Roman customs were adopted in the conquered countries. Buildings and architecture, engineering, town planning, clothing, language, law, education – all these were modelled on Roman examples. People throughout the Roman Empire shared a common way of life, from Africa to Britain, and from Syria to Spain. This is why the history of Rome plays a part in the history of many other countries.

Many of the places in this book are in towns and cities, because the Romans, like other people in the ancient world, were tremendously proud of their towns and the facilities in them. Some of the places in the book are connected with the army, because the army played a large part in Roman life – not just because it conquered foreign countries, but because it was also a force in Roman politics. Other places are in the countryside, because both the cities and the army depended on the country for supplies of food. In the following pages you can find out more about places like these which were important in the Roman way of life.

THE FORUM

The Forum was a public square in the city of Rome. To live nearby was to be at the heart of city life. A writer who lived in the first century after the birth of Christ (AD) tells a story about a new house built close to the Forum for a great Roman soldier and politician named Marius:

'When Marius came back to Rome, a house was built for him near the Forum. He selected the site so people who wanted to see him would not have far to walk.'

This mosaic shows a group of writers and thinkers who have gathered to discuss the news and ideas of the day. Many Romans used to meet like this in the Forum. It was the heart of city life.

The centre of a city

As Rome grew from a small settlement on the hills above the River Tiber, people decided to set aside a special place which they could use for trade, religious gatherings and many other different kinds of meeting. This place became known as the Forum. Historians believe that the first Forum in Rome developed around 800 BC.

The remains of many Roman monuments still survive in the Forum in Rome today. Here you can see part of a temple, with a triumphal arch behind. In the background you can see the Colosseum, a great amphitheatre. Throughout the Empire, architects and builders modelled their work on buildings like these.

The centre of many cities

The power of Rome grew. By about 270 BC, most of the Italian mainland had been conquered by the Romans. A successful war with the people of Carthage (in modern-day Tunisia) made Rome the greatest power in the Mediterranean, and from this time on its influence grew. By the time of the death of the Emperor Trajan in AD 117, Roman power stretched from Spain and North Africa to Britain, parts of Germany and Asia Minor. The countries Rome conquered adopted many parts of the Roman way of life, and in this way many cities came to have their own forum. A Roman writer called Tacitus describes how this happened when Britain was conquered by the Romans in AD 43. He is writing about the Roman Governor, Agricola: '*His aim was to make the people used to a life without war, and so he encouraged them to build public squares and houses.*'

The writing of a great Roman architect, Vitruvius, tells us how a forum like this was laid out, with colonnades (covered walkways) running round the sides of the square, and space for a temple, basilica (town hall) and other buildings. Archaeologists have discovered that many such squares (fora) were planned in this way, from Timgad in Africa (in modern-day Algeria) to Pompeii in Italy.

A centre of power

The forum was the centre of political life in many cities. In Rome it was the setting for all sorts of political activities, such as debates about who should rule the Roman people and decisions about how to uphold law and order. One contemporary tells us that at the time of the first emperor, Augustus (31 BC–AD 14), so many cases were brought before the law courts that the Forum could not hold them all.

Monuments that speak

The buildings and monuments erected in the Forum in Rome also tell us about its importance in struggles for political power. One of these was a stone platform called the 'rostra'. Many Roman leaders and politicians addressed their subjects from the rostra. But there were other ways for them to communicate with the people, such as the building of impressive monuments. In AD 113 the Emperor Trajan ordered that a 30 metre column showing a spiral of pictures illustrating his victories over the people of Dacia (in modern-day Romania) should be erected in the Forum. This was intended to make his achievements known to everyone who saw it. Many Roman leaders had monuments of this kind created for the Forum. Such monuments had a message for the people of the time – and today they tell the story of the past.

This painting shows actors and one of the masks worn during a performance. The Roman architect, Vitruvius, tells us that plays brought crowds flocking to the Forum. Many other activities took place there as well.

Bankers, actors, gladiators

Many other activities took place in the Forum. Vitruvius describes some of these: banking, storing money, meetings between people and politicians, theatrical performances, and fights between gladiators. His list makes it clear that the Forum was at the centre of public life. You can find out more about the Roman way of life in the rest of this book.

THE HOUSEHOLD

St Augustine (AD 354–430), a great Christian thinker who came from Africa, explains that the household was an important part of Roman life:

'The house is part of the city, and the father who rules the household takes his rules from the laws of the city.'

The family and others

St Augustine wrote these words in the fifth century AD. It was a time when Roman power in Western Europe was growing weaker. But although the family arrangements that St Augustine describes were also starting to change, they had affected the way people lived for many centuries.

A Roman ring showing the heads of a married couple. When a marriage took place, the woman was transferred from her father's authority to the power of her new husband's family.

The Roman household described by St Augustine was much larger than most households today. It sometimes contained several generations of the same family – grand-parents, parents and children (even adult children) – as well as other people like servants and slaves who worked in the house. The wealthier the family, the more people there were. In the homes of important men and women, there was also a constant stream of visitors and people who came to ask for favours and advice. Many would arrive each morning, a large crowd gathering outside and waiting to be let in. In return for help and gifts, these people gave support to the family if it was needed. Special words described this relationship: great men acted as 'patrons' and the people who came to them were 'clients'.

The days of ghosts

The Romans believed that the dead were still important members of the household. Each household had a place

Every Roman household contained a shrine like this, dedicated to the household gods.

for a special shrine called the 'lararium'. Here prayers were said and offerings were made to gods known as the lares. The lares were the spirits of dead ancestors who were believed to watch over the household. Religious festivals took place during the year to honour the lares and the spirits of the dead. One of the most important was the festival of the Lemuria – the 'days of ghosts' – which took place in May.

Living up to the past

Roman people believed that it was their duty to respect family history and live up to the example of their ancestors. It was common for statues or pictures of important members of the family to be placed in the household shrine when they had died. A man who came to Rome in about 200 BC describes this: *'After the burial, the Romans put a portrait of the deceased in the most important part of the house. It is contained in a small shrine made of wood.*' Seeing these portraits and statues reminded the Romans of their duty to the past.

Part of government

The household was ruled by a man called the 'paterfamilias'. This old Latin word means 'father of the household'. When Romans used the word, they were not describing the type of family relationship we know today. For them, the father of the household meant a man to whom the law gave special power over all the people living in his home: wife, children, the slaves and servants alike. The power given to the father of the household was part of the overall way in which Roman society was ruled. You can see this more clearly by looking at some of his rights and responsibilities.

A scene from family life, showing a Roman father and son. Even as adults, Romans were expected to behave with great respect towards their parents.

Powers of life and death

The authority of the paterfamilias was very great. He had the power of life and death over his wife, slaves and children and could condemn them to death if they committed a crime. Adult children were also under their father's power – even if they married and had children of their own. The father arranged marriages for his children and controlled their finances for as long as he lived.

The Roman writer, Suetonius, tells us that the Emperor Augustus (see page 9) adopted a young man named Tiberius so that there would be someone to succeed him as emperor. This meant that Tiberius came under his new father's power, even though he was at this time old enough to be an experienced soldier.

THE KITCHEN

Here a Roman lawyer and official named Pliny the Younger (*c.* AD 61–113) describes a meal which had been prepared in his kitchens:

'A lettuce each, snails, eggs, wine served with honey and cooled with snow, olives, beetroots, gherkins and other dishes.'

At work in the kitchen

In wealthy households, food was prepared by slaves or cooks who were specially hired for great occasions. They worked together in the hot, smoky kitchen. Food was cooked on small charcoal fires laid on top of a hearth at waist level.

Here you can see a shop selling poultry, pork and other types of meat. Pictures of everyday life like this can be found on the stones and monuments that were erected on Roman graves.

THE KITCHEN

As you can see from Pliny's dinner menu, the Romans ate a wide variety of different foods. Many of the foods they ate are ones with which we are familiar today. Meat – such as beef, venison, boar, poultry and game – was roasted or stewed. Many people liked fish; a list written by a writer in the first century AD tells us that fish eaten at this time included tunny fish, oysters, dolphin, pike, turbot and lamprey. Fish were sometimes bred and raised in fish farms ready to be sold to cooks for the kitchen. In Rome, vegetables like cucumber, garlic, lettuce, onion, cabbage, artichokes and asparagus were available. So too were olives, apples, grapes, dates and other fruits.

But there are differences between Roman cooking and modern cooking. For example, feasts at the tables of the most wealthy Roman citizens might include dormouse, flamingo-tongues, peacock-brains, ostrich, parrot or donkey. The Romans also liked extremely strong sauces, such as garum, made from fermented fish.

The eruption of Mount Vesuvius in AD 79 preserved the Roman town of Pompeii in Italy just as it was when its inhabitants lived there. This is the kitchen of one of the houses, with pots set out on the raised hearth, ready for a meal to be cooked.

Food of the poor

This type of food was eaten by the wealthy. The poor had a much simpler diet. We can find out more about what the poor ate by reading the words of a writer named Suetonius, who was born around the year AD 69. Suetonius tells us that coarse bread, fish, cheese and figs were the foods eaten by the 'common people'.

At one time, all the people of Rome had eaten foods like these. At the very beginnings of Roman history, when the Romans were peasant farmers rather than city dwellers, the diet of most people was plain and unvaried. Many meals at this time took the form of a thick porridge called 'puls', served with lentils, peas, beans or green vegetables.

Food gradually became more and more elaborate – and began to create bitter arguments. Some Romans opposed the new eating habits and longed for a return to the old days of 'puls' and lentils. This is what one contemporary had to say about the question: *'Shell-fish have contributed greatly to slipping standards and extravagant ways of life.'* Surprising as it sounds, this writer clearly believed that elaborate and expensive foods were a sign that the people of Rome were living beyond their means. He was not the only one to express views like this.

Paintings like this, which were rich in accurate detail, were popular with the Romans. This was a new tradition in painting. Many non-Roman people, like the Celts, had created works of art with swirling patterns and fabulous animals and birds. For them, the Roman style was new and different.

Bread and circuses

The supply of food came to play an important part in struggles for power in Rome. The population grew quickly as people moved into the city. Many newcomers found no work, and lived in poverty. Fearing that the poor would turn to violence and throw them from power, politicians courted popularity by ordering regular distributions of free food. This practice was introduced by a politician named Gaius Gracchus, who died in 121 BC. A story told by Suetonius will show you exactly why politicians were fearful: *'Bad weather led to a shortage of corn in Rome. The Emperor was cornered in the Forum by a mob who rained stale bread and threats upon him.'*

Free entertainment was also provided for the people of Rome. The poet Juvenal (AD 60–140) describes how people lost interest in politics once this happened. He sums matters up like this: *'They want only two things – bread and circuses.'*

THE CITY

Towards the beginning of the first century AD, a man left his home in the city of Rome to travel through part of the Roman Empire. He was the poet, Ovid. His writing describes how he missed life in the city:

'I remember that beautiful town, the fora, the temples, the theatres of marble, the pools and canals.'

The only way to live

Many people at this time would have felt as Ovid did. As far as the Romans were concerned, a city was the only place to live. The history of the modern word 'civilization' tells us a great deal about this belief. It comes from Latin words meaning 'city' and 'citizen'. For the Romans, and for other ancient peoples like the Greeks, city life *was* civilization – anything else was the life of a savage or barbarian.

The inhabitants of cities at this time were tremendously proud of the environment in which they lived. The emperors and leading citizens paid for fine villas, roads, aqueducts, bridges and other buildings. This tomb has carvings of some of the buildings erected in Rome in the first century AD.

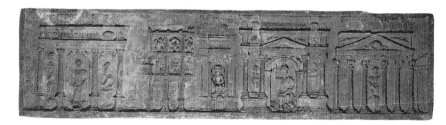

A story told by a first-century writer named Plutarch will help you see this more clearly. Plutarch explains how bands of pirates had terrorized the Mediterranean, attacking sailors at sea and raiding the countryside. A soldier and politician named Pompey was sent from Rome to capture the pirates. Plutarch's words tell us what happened next. Pompey *'sent the men from the sea to the land so they would try civilized life and become used to living in cities'*. This story shows Roman belief in the importance of city life.

The inhabitants of Rome naturally believed that Rome was the best of all cities, but they were agreed that life in any city at all was far, far better than life elsewhere.

A town with high walls built around it. Outside the town you can see the countryside dotted with villas – the country houses of wealthy Romans.

Building cities

The Romans encouraged city life throughout the Empire. In some places, such as the East, city life was already strong. In others, especially in Celtic countries like Britain and Gaul (modern-day France), it was a new development. Under the Romans, many new cities were built. Some were built as 'colonies', cities inhabited by retired soldiers. Timgad in the mountains of Algeria was one of these. Some developed out of forts and military settlements, such as Ostia (in Italy), and others grew out of sites which had been important before the Romans arrived, such as Paris (in modern-day France). A great many of these cities were planned and laid out to a standard design. The forum stood at the centre of the city, with a temple, basilica and other offices. Streets ran in a grid pattern on all sides of the forum. Here were shops, houses and other buildings. Many cities in the western part of the Roman Empire were surrounded by high walls to give protection to the inhabitants. This was especially common from the second and third centuries AD onwards.

Public places

The architect Vitruvius describes the different types of building to be found in Roman cities: markets, baths, theatres, temples and fora. Vitruvius' list shows that many of the important places in the city were designed for everyone to use; for the Romans life in the city was a sociable business. Today public buildings like those Vitruvius lists survive from cities all over the old Empire. Among the greatest examples are the Pantheon (temple) built for the Emperor Hadrian (AD 117–138) in Rome, and the Cluny Baths in Paris. The style and grandeur of Roman buildings like these have impressed and influenced people ever since.

This model of a Roman apartment block has been made by examining the remains of buildings which survive from this time.

The Romans took many ideas from other ancient people, such as the Greeks and the Etruscans. From the Etruscans they learned many techniques that were useful for building sewers, roads and bridges. From the Greeks they took the idea of a carefully planned city with a checkerboard pattern of streets. The Romans also developed techniques of their own: for example, they often used arches in building work.

Private places

Cities were noisy and full of life. In Rome itself, the population grew fast and poorer people had difficulty in finding housing. Tall tenement blocks of flats, four or five storeys high, were built to try to ease the problem. '*In this way, with many floors high in the air, the Roman people can find places to live*', writes Vitruvius. The tenements were overcrowded, and there was always the danger of fire breaking out and spreading rapidly from one flat to another.

THE BATHS

O ne day an inhabitant of the Roman city of Timgad in Africa (in modern-day Algeria) found he had nothing to do. Picking up a sharp implement, he idly scratched some words on the stone paving in the middle of town. As far as he was concerned, he was just passing the time. Today his message tells us about one of the most popular of all Roman occupations – going to the baths:

'Hunting, bathing, playing, laughing – they're what life is about.'

Going to the baths

We know nothing about the Roman who wrote this graffiti, apart from his enthusiasm for the baths – an enthusiasm shared throughout the whole Roman world. Baths were built for the army, by wealthy citizens for their private houses and, above all, for the cities: in around 100 BC there were more than 150 public baths in the city of Rome alone. Wherever the Romans travelled, this part of their way of life went with them.

There were many reasons why people went to the baths. One was to keep clean, but there were many others, too. The baths were a place to relax and meet friends. Many were elaborate complexes of buildings. Some contained a gymnasium for sport and exercise, gardens, covered walkways, libraries, meeting halls, rooms where food and drink were sold, and plenty of corners to sit and talk.

The baths were usually packed with people. As well as the bathers who came crowding in to enjoy themselves each afternoon and evening, there were also many people who worked at the baths. There were

About 1,900 years ago, this glass bottle for perfume was made in Syria. Visitors to the Roman baths had their skin rubbed with special oils as part of the bathing process.

This picture shows what it must have been like to take a plunge at the Baths of Caracalla in Rome. Can you see the statues and the ornate columns? The Baths were also decorated with mosaics showing wrestlers and other scenes.

slaves to stoke the furnaces which provided heating, slaves to check that the water was the correct temperature, slaves to look after towels and linen, some who worked in the dressing rooms, and many others. The baths were places where money was to be made: visitors bought snacks such as sausages, drinks and pastries; took part in gambling competitions; paid for massages and hair cuts.

A vivid description of a visit to the baths was written in the first century AD by a writer called Seneca:

'There is every kind of noise here. I hear the gasps of people exercising with weights, the slapping sound of someone being massaged. Then someone playing ball turns up and cries out the score, and another starts a noisy quarrel.'

An architect's view

Roman baths were more like sauna baths than modern baths. Our knowledge of how the baths were built, and

how they worked, comes from the writings of contemporary architects like Vitruvius, and from looking at the buildings themselves. Such evidence tells us that the baths consisted of a series of rooms heated to different temperatures – hot, warm and cold – through which the visitor passed. In the hot room, the 'caldarium', the bather worked up a sweat. This was meant to bring dirt to the surface of the skin. Then the body was treated with special oils and the dirt scraped off with a metal instrument called a 'strigil'. The next room was the 'tepidarium', which was a little cooler. Lastly the bather visited the 'frigidarium', the cold bath, for a plunge in a cold pool.

The baths used water brought through aqueducts (special stone channels that carried water), like the one which supplied the Antonine Baths in Carthage (in North Africa). To produce the range of different temperatures required, heat from a furnace was drawn underneath the floors of the baths.

A picture of slaves busy working with metal, together with some of their tools and finished products. Slaves were to be found working almost everywhere. At the baths there were many jobs for them to do, looking after the buildings and seeing to the needs of the bathers.

Baths in muddy water

Roman bathing habits changed over time. In the first century AD, when Seneca wrote his account, baths were decorated with marble panels, mosaics and statues. Some baths in Rome could hold more than 1,500 people. Before this time, baths were much simpler. Seneca tells us that Scipio, a great soldier who died in 184 BC, hardly noticed if his bath water was muddy. This would not have satisfied bathers in Seneca's day!

THE COUNTRYSIDE

Here the poet Virgil (70–19 BC) describes how Roman farmers tried to make sure their fields would produce good crops – by worshipping Ceres, goddess of the harvest:

> *When spring is coming, let your labourers*
>   *worship Ceres,*
> *Take a beast to be sacrificed three times*
> *Round the growing crops …*

Praying to the gods for rain

When you know that another piece of advice Virgil had for the farmers involved praying to the gods for rain, you will see that many superstitions and religious beliefs influenced life and work in the countryside. Many gods and goddesses were thought to have power over farming and the countryside. They included Bacchus, the god of wine; Pan, who watched over animals and shepherds; and Flora, the goddess of flowers.

This scene shows shepherds at work with sheep in the countryside. In his poem The Georgics, *Virgil had plenty of advice for shepherds and everyone else involved in Roman farming.*

Remembering life on the land

The first people of Rome were peasant farmers, and the farming way of life was remembered by Romans for many centuries. When Rome had become a powerful city, its citizens still celebrated religious festivals concerned with the harvest. Remembering the old farming life, some people even suggested that it was better than modern ways – less extravagant and more hard-working.

In fact, life on the land had changed a great deal since the days when the first peasant farmers lived on the hills of Rome. The Latin tribes who settled here were especially interested in keeping herds of cattle, a type of farming called 'pastoral agriculture'. For these people, cattle meant wealth. 'Pecunia', the word the Romans later used for 'money', came from the word for cattle, a reminder of those early days. As well as keeping animals, farmers also grew crops (this is called arable farming) and harvested them. These farmers worked on a small scale, providing food for their own needs.

Country life was a very popular subject for mosaics. This one was made for the home of a wealthy Roman. But Roman influence did not bring great changes to the way people actually lived and worked in the countryside.

From small farms to large estates

One of the most important changes in the way of life in the countryside involved those who lived and worked on the land. Until the time of the Second Punic War (a great war fought in 218–202 BC between the Romans and the people of Carthage in North Africa), Italy had been a country of large and small estates, or farms. But this changed when the war ended. Small farmers, whose land had been damaged in the war, left to try a new life in the city. The large estates took over the lands of those who left and became larger still. Such estates were known as 'latifundia'. They were owned by wealthy families. Many preferred to live in town and appoint a manager to run the estate for them, with slaves to do the work. From time to time they visited and spent a few days relaxing in one of their villas (country houses), but they were rarely involved in day to day farming. Farming had now become a profitable business instead of a family way of life.

Grain being loaded on to a ship. Rome's population grew fast, and people there came to depend on supplies of corn being brought to the city. Free food was regularly distributed to the people.

Feeding the towns

The Roman countryside fed the towns with the crops and livestock it produced. The city of Rome was especially dependent on supplies of food being brought in to feed its million inhabitants. Grain from Sicily, Egypt and Africa made great contributions. A Jewish writer named Josephus, who lived in the first century AD, describes how many people believed that, *'Because of its corn, Egypt was the most important part of the Empire.'* Peace throughout the Empire meant that foodstuffs and other goods could be transported in safety from country to town, and from one part of the Empire to another. You can see this in the story of the island of Britain, conquered by the Romans in AD 43. Even before it was conquered, Britain had provided the Romans with agricultural products such as cattle, corn and animal hides.

THE VILLA

In the first century AD, a Roman named Pliny the Younger wanted to tell a friend about a holiday he had recently taken. To do this, he described the villa (country house) at which he had stayed:

'The villa opens into a hall. Then there is a courtyard surrounded by colonnades, and an inner hall. Behind this lies the dining-room, which looks out towards the sea.

Villas like this were built in many parts of the Roman Empire.

Working farms and small palaces

Not all villas were the same. Some were working farms, built at the heart of a country estate, complete with barns, stables, hen-houses, stalls for cattle and oxen, and room for the slaves who worked the land. Others were elaborate country houses built close enough to town for their owners to take holidays there. Villas of this sort were more like small palaces than farms. The Emperor Hadrian's villa at Tivoli, near Rome, is a good example. Built in the second century AD, it took almost 12 years to complete. It contained suites of baths, a library, court-yards, lakes and gardens, and it was decorated with statues, mosaics and wall paintings. A villa like this was designed for a luxurious

Here you can see the richly painted walls of a villa. Every sort of luxury was to be found in a villa like this, from under-floor heating, to magnificent furnishings made of bronze.

way of life. Some even had sophisticated under-floor heating systems called 'hypocausts'. Hot air from a furnace passed into a space beneath the floors, heating the rooms above.

Villas and their owners

Villas were owned by many different kinds of people. Some were owned by important government officials, like Pliny the Younger. Pliny also worked as a lawyer. He was a wealthy man and owned several villas. Many villa-owners came from backgrounds like his.

In the provinces of the Roman Empire, some villas were owned by families which had been powerful before the Romans conquered their country. Historians believe that the villa at Fishbourne in Sussex (England) might have a story like this. This villa was very fine. It was first made of timber, and then rebuilt in stone soon after the country was invaded by the Emperor Claudius in AD 43. The site was very large, spreading over more than 4 hectares. The villa contained a suite of baths, and a special chamber where the owner could receive people who came to make requests. Luxury building materials were used, such as marble from Italy. The size of the villa, the functions of the different rooms and the grandeur of the buildings are all signs that the owner was a person of great importance. But who was

The owners of villas were some of the wealthiest people in Roman society. This painting of a garden, for example, was made to decorate a villa used by Livia, the wife of the Emperor Augustus.

he? Although they cannot be sure, many historians think that the owner was a man named Cogidubnus, who had been powerful before the Romans took power and then ruled the area on their behalf.

Living a Roman life in the country

The owners of the villa at Fishbourne, whoever they were, had one thing in common with villa-owners in Italy and others throughout the Roman Empire: they were all living a Roman life in the country. The Romans encouraged the people they conquered, particularly the chiefs and other leaders, to follow Roman customs. There were political reasons for this. It was felt that sharing a common way of life would increase the ties of loyalty between Rome and the provinces, so that there would be less likelihood of rebellion breaking out. In the first century AD, the historian Tacitus summed it up like this: *'The Britons think of these things as civilization. In fact they are a sign that they have been conquered.'*

The remains of the villa built for the Emperor Hadrian at Tivoli in Italy. This grand scale of building came to an end when Roman power was threatened by raids from enemy tribes, and when trade and prosperity began to suffer.

Beginnings and ends

Villas had been built in Italy from about 200 BC. They continued to be built for many centuries. One contemporary describes building work at a villa in the province of Gaul (modern-day France) in the fifth century AD. But by this time, villa life was coming to an end. The outlook for trade and agriculture was unsettled, and the peace of the Empire was disturbed by the raids of Germanic tribes. Villa life depended on peace, prosperity and trade – and these things had gone.

THE VINEYARD

Italy was famous for its vineyards – plots of land on which grapes were grown to make wine. In a long poem about farming customs called *The Georgics*, the poet Virgil describes how a vineyard should be laid out:

> *Draw up your vineyard in regular lines*
> *The plants like rows of soldiers;*
> *Thus the earth may nourish all,*
> *And the branches have room to spread.*

A land of vineyards

For the Romans, growing vines and making wine were especially profitable types of farming. Some estates, for example in the Campania area of Italy, specialized in vine-growing because of the large sums of money to be made from it. According to a writer who lived in the first century AD, *'Campania has great quantities of corn, vines and olives.'* Many estates in this area produced wine on a large scale. One particularly famous example is the Villa Boscoreale, the farming headquarters of a great estate producing wine and olive

A ship holding barrels of wine is rowed down river. There was a great deal of long-distance trade in wine in the ancient world.

oil. Our knowledge about Boscoreale comes from archaeology. Archaeology gives us evidence about the use to which different parts of the villa were put. At Boscoreale there was a room for the wine-press, a cellar where wine was stored in special earthenware jars, and accommodation for slaves and other workers. The message from Boscoreale is that wine-production was an extremely important source of income on the estate. There were many villas like Boscoreale, where farming was strictly organized and run as a business venture.

A servant in return for a drink

Wine was one of the main drinks at this time: from about 100 BC and in the first century AD there was much trade in Italian wine. Farms like the Villa Boscoreale supplied customers in foreign countries as well as those at home in Italy. Ship-loads of wine were sent abroad – especially to the Celtic nobility of Gaul (modern-day France) and Britain. One contemporary writer records the high price which the Gauls were prepared to pay: *'For one amphora* [jar] *of wine … a slave; that is a servant in return for a drink!'* Most merchants and wine-producers had to be content with a price lower than this.

Here you can see workers taking part in the grape harvest. Baskets of fruit are brought to be pressed, to release their juice. How is the pressing done? Are machines involved?

Even the government was interested in the wine trade. For a number of years it gave orders that provinces such as Africa and Transalpine Gaul were not to grow vines. This arrangement was intended to help Italian vine-growers.

Growing crops and finding customers

Vine-growing was not the only type of farming where profits were to be made. Some Italian farmers specialized in growing olives, which were harvested and pressed to produce olive oil. Like wine, olive oil

Too much wine leads to a quarrel! Wine was the most popular drink at this time, and many farms were involved in large-scale production.

was exported to many different countries. Late in the first century AD, this began to change. More foreign wine and olive oil were produced and Italian farmers lost customers. Because of this some farmers decided to grow different crops – such as cherries, apples and pears – instead. For cereal crops like wheat, Rome came to rely more and more on supplies from places overseas like Sicily and Africa.

Money and honour

Only one kind of physical work was thought suitable for Roman citizens: farming. It was seen as the only honourable way for a Roman to make money. Many of the most wealthy and learned people of the time came to be interested in agriculture, and some also wrote about the subject. The work of writers like these tells us a great deal about Roman crops, livestock, tools and farming customs. The writer Pliny the Elder, who lived in the first century AD, describes how many people kept bees for honey. Some of the tasks he describes are still carried out by bee-keepers today. This is what he says about honey: *'There are three sorts of honey. One is spring honey, which is called flower honey. One is summer honey. The third is "heath honey" which is made in autumn when heather is the only plant to flower.'*

THE ROAD

Rome was famous for its network of well-constructed roads. Here a politician who lived in the first century BC tells a friend the best route to take for a journey from Rome to the south of Italy:

'I suggest that you come by the Appian Way, and make haste to me at Brundisium.'

Roads to Rome

A great system of roads connected the city of Rome first with important sites in Italy and later with different parts of the Empire. This was extremely unusual for the time. Roads had been built for the rulers of Persia (modern-day Iran) around 500 BC, and also by the Etruscans, a people who had dominated large parts of Italy between the eighth and the fourth centuries BC. The Romans learned a great deal from their techniques, and some Roman roads followed the routes of the roads the Etruscans had laid out earlier.

The first great Roman road to be built was the Via

This photograph shows part of a Roman road, the Via Sacra (Sacred Way) in Rome. Peaceful conditions in the Roman Empire enabled travellers to pass from one land to another.

Appia (Appian Way) – the road referred to at the beginning of this chapter – which led from Rome to Capua. Work on the road began in 312 BC. Other Roman roads joined together important ports and cities. Among the most famous are the Via Aurelia, which led to Pisa, and the Via Flaminia, which led to Rimini.

As the Roman Empire grew, roads were built to provide communications with cities further away. The Via Aurelia was extended to Gaul (modern-day France) so that traders, messengers, government officials and armies could travel easily between Gaul and Rome. Many other countries were connected to Rome by road.

The road-makers

Many roads were built by skilled members of the Roman army. Here is an account of road-makers in the Roman army that was written in the first century AD: '*Next came the road-makers. Their work was to make the roads straight and make uneven tracks level so that the army could march easily.*'

The first task was to survey the land. Everything was very carefully planned so that the road ran in as straight a line as possible. To build a road, two ditches were dug about 7½ metres apart, and then the top soil

The remains of Roman footwear found by archaeologists. Wealthy Romans wore boots when they were outside. In the house they were changed for sandals.

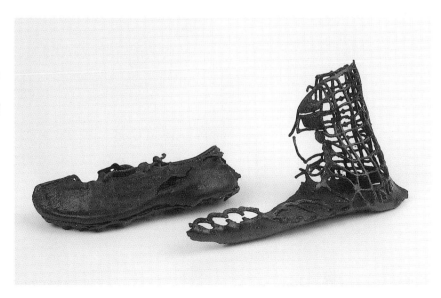

was removed until a firm base was reached. Layers of sand and chalk were piled on this base, then large stones fixed with cement or clay, then a mixture of chalk and gravel, and finally the surface of stones or pebbles. The surface was curved slightly so that rain-water could run away. Roman road-building techniques were not matched in Western Europe until very recent times, and many roads, like the Fosse Way in England, still follow the course of old Roman roads.

Vast sums of money

Building roads and keeping them in good condition was expensive. One contemporary tells us that it took 'vast sums of money' to look after the Via Appia alone. Some of the expense was met by the government. But wealthy citizens were encouraged to take an interest in building and maintaining roads, too. Road names sometimes give us clues about this. For example, the Via Appia was named after Appius Claudius, a high-ranking government official who worked to promote the road. Accounts written by people who lived at the time also describe how Roman citizens came to be involved. The Roman historian, Suetonius, explains that the Emperor Augustus *'improved the roads leading to Rome. He repaved the Via Flaminia with his own money and encouraged soldiers who had won triumphs to spend their prize money on the roads.'* In the provinces, the people conquered by Rome had to contribute towards the cost of building roads through their land, as well as providing labourers to build them.

Milestones like this were set up at intervals along Roman roads to show the distance between towns. (A mile is about 1½ kilometres.) In the Forum in Rome, a milestone called the 'Golden Milestone' recorded the distance between Rome and the most important cities of the Empire.

From the fourth century AD, Roman power in Western Europe gave way under economic problems and the invasion of tribes like the Franks and Goths. There was less money to spend on maintaining roads, and there was also less peaceful travel from one land to another.

THE SHRINE

A merchant who lived in the Roman town of Carlisle in England had the words of this vow cut on a stone which still survives:

'To the mother goddesses, I dedicate this shrine. Bring me good fortune and I will paint these letters in gold.'

The Romans worshipped many different gods, goddesses and spirits. Shrines (small places beside which people worshipped) played an important part in their religion. Each shrine was dedicated to a particular god or goddess and was thought to be its home.

Watching over every part of life

Each god was believed to watch over a different part of life. The chief Roman gods were Jupiter and Juno. Jupiter was the lord of light and weather. Juno was the goddess of the moon and the night sky, and of women. Jupiter and Juno had been worshipped in Rome from at least 500 BC. There were many other Roman gods, from Mars (god of war and agriculture) and Vesta (goddess of the hearth and home), to Mercury (god of trade and wealth).

Roman people believed that the gods played a part in everything that happened, from birth to death. These models of parts of the body were made in the hope that the gods would bring them good health.

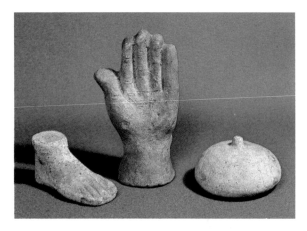

Honouring the gods

Shrines were set up in many different places: in the home, in towns, in the countryside – even in military forts. They were treated with great respect, and special religious ceremonies took place to honour the gods who were believed to watch over them. You can see this if we look at the shrines built at city crossroads. These were dedicated to the gods of the cross-

roads, who were thought to watch over the local community. Each year a festival known as the Compitalia was held as a sign of devotion to these gods. The Emperor Augustus (see page 9) encouraged this. The writer Suetonius describes how Augustus '*ordered that the figures of the gods should be decorated with spring and summer flowers*'.

Beliefs old and new

As the Romans conquered different lands, they learned about the gods worshipped by other people. The Greeks, for instance, worshipped gods such as Pluto, god of the underworld. The Celtic lands, like Britain and Gaul (modern-day France), had their own gods and beliefs. Many were linked to springs, streams, lakes, woods and other natural features which were believed to be the homes of gods. Beliefs of this kind were similar to the Romans' beliefs. The Romans added many of them to their own religion. Many of the gods of Greece were included in this way.

Sometimes the Romans changed the names of deities (gods) worshipped in foreign lands. This happened at Bath, in England, where the Britons had worshipped a goddess named Sulis. The Romans who conquered the

A procession of people going to take part in a religious ceremony. Look at the way the faces have been carved. The Romans took great pains to make their paintings and sculpture look as life-like as possible.

area also decided to worship Sulis, but they renamed her 'Sulis Minerva' after the Roman goddess, Minerva.

From one land to another

Many religious beliefs were spread as soldiers, traders, government officials and their families travelled from one land to another. Worship of the Persian (Iranian) god, Mithras, spread like this, and so did Christianity. Archaeology tells us a great deal about how religious ideas travelled round the Empire. Objects and religious inscriptions found near Hadrian's Wall in the north of England, for example, show us the wide range of gods that were worshipped by the Roman soldiers there. These included the Roman gods, Mars and Minerva; the Celtic horse goddess, Epona; the Persian god, Mithras; and local gods like Silvanus, god of hunting.

This picture shows troops leading animals to be sacrificed to the gods. The word 'sacrifice' means to make something holy by giving it to the gods.

Signs and superstitions

Many superstitions affected everyday life. According to Suetonius, the Emperor Augustus was terrified of storms and carried a piece of seal-skin as a charm against them. People at this time also believed that the gods sent signs of events to come. The Roman writer, Livy (59 BC–AD 17), lists some of these when he writes: *'In Cumae, the statue of Apollo wept. In Rome it rained blood.'* Signs of this sort might be interpreted as warnings that an important man was about to die, or that the army would be unsuccessful in battle.

THE FORT

These words were cut in stone to record building work at a Roman fort near Hadrian's Wall in the north of England in the third century AD:

'The commander's house, which was overgrown, and the headquarters buildings were restored under the direction of Flavius Martinus the Centurion.'

Shelter for the army

Shelter had to be provided for the army when it was on campaign. Camps, forts and fortresses were built for this purpose. Camps were built as temporary shelters for the army at the end of a day's march. Forts and fortresses provided more permanent accommodation. They were all meticulously planned complexes of buildings. Forts were usually the base for a single army unit, often a unit of auxiliary troops (men from the Roman provinces who fought in the Roman army, but who were not Roman citizens). Fortresses were large establishments built to house a legion.

Making camp

Precise rules set out how the soldiers were to make camp. The first-century writer, Josephus, paints a vivid picture of the Romans' methods: *'Uneven ground is made level and a rectangular-shaped site laid out. Walls, towers and four gates, one in each wall, are built. The camp is marked out in streets, the commander's tent and the headquarters at the centre.'* Other contemporary accounts, together with the work of modern archaeologists, show us that the scene Josephus describes was not at all unusual. Camps were made in this way wherever the Roman army went on

This is a statue of Hercules, a hero who played an important part in Greek legend. It was found in the North of England. This shows us how ideas and religious beliefs spread throughout the Roman Empire. They were often carried by Roman soldiers.

campaign – from Judaea (the area around Jerusalem) to Scotland.

Each camp was fortified for protection. A ditch was dug around the outside, and earth or turfs were then piled up to create a bank. On top of this, a wall of wooden stakes was erected. Each soldier carried two stakes as part of his equipment for this purpose. Inside the camp, tents were put up as shelter. These too were arranged according to strict rules, in lines marked out by surveyors.

From camps to forts

The Roman soldier not only had to know how to handle his weapons – he also had to be able to handle tools for building, such as a spade or a pick. Here you can see Hadrian's Wall, built by Roman soldiers.

From about the time of Julius Caesar's campaigns in Gaul (modern-day France), around 55 BC, the army began to build more permanent bases. These were required for a number of reasons. One was to give better protection from the weather, especially in winter. In earlier years Roman armies often withdrew to a nearby town for the winter. Now that they were

involved in campaigns in North West Europe, away from the warm climate of the Mediterranean, good winter shelter became very important. Permanent army bases like forts and fortresses were created for another reason, too. Some areas of the Empire, such as Scotland, the north of England and parts of Germany, were not easy or quick to conquer. Soldiers had to be stationed near trouble zones like these for many years in order to drive off attacks. Permanent bases, like the fortresses at York and Chester in England, were provided for these men. Timber buildings replaced the earlier leather tents. In time this too changed, stone buildings replacing timber from about the end of the first century AD. But for all these changes, the organization and lay-out of forts and fortresses were still much the same as those of the early marching camps.

Towns in miniature

Inside a fort or fortress, a wide range of buildings catered for the soldiers' needs. These included rows of barracks for the troops, granaries for storing corn, stables, a bath-house, hospital and work shops. Josephus describes a camp as a town which sprang up overnight: '*It is like a town with streets, a market-place, room for craftsmen and officers.*' All these buildings were erected by the soldiers themselves. One Roman soldier sent to the East records his dislike of jobs like this: '*I thank the gods that as an officer I stroll about while others work all day cutting stones.*'

A town sometimes grew up outside the fort as traders flocked to sell their goods to the soldiers, setting up shops and inns, and the wives and families of the troops settled nearby. A settlement like this was called a 'vicus'. Settlements developed at Housesteads on Hadrian's Wall in England, Trier in Germany and many other parts of the Empire.

Here you can see an altar found in a Roman fort. It was dedicated to the 'discipline of the emperor'. Discipline in the army was very harsh, and soldiers were punished with beatings.

THE HOSPITAL

Early in the second century AD, new bedding was required at a hospital in the Roman province of Cappadocia (modern-day East Anatolia, in Turkey). An order was placed for more:

'For the hospital, one blanket, plain white, in wool.'

Inside a Roman hospital

To find out about Roman hospitals, we need to study the work of archaeologists and documents written by people who lived at the time. These sources of evidence show us that Roman hospitals fell into two different categories: hospitals built for the army in forts and fortresses, and hospitals built for civilians in towns and cities. Little is known about civilian hospitals, but historians believe that they were built to the same plan as military hospitals. Let's look more closely at some of these military hospitals and see what they tell us.

Archaeologists have discovered where military hospitals once stood in many different parts of the Roman Empire: in the legionary fortresses at Inchtuthil in Scotland, and Castel Vetera (modern-day Xanten) on the River Rhine in Germany, for example. Like many Roman buildings, hospitals were designed to a standard plan. A rectangular court-yard lay at the centre of each hospital site. This provided peace and fresh air. The hospital buildings were ranged round the four sides of the court-yard, with a corridor which ran round all four sides so that doctors and patients could walk round the entire hospital. Small wards led off this corridor. There was also an operating theatre where operations like amputations took place. Some hospitals, such as Castel Vetera, even had their own bath-houses. These things are signs that the Romans

At this time, many people mistrusted the work of doctors. They looked for cures in religion and traditional customs. A Roman who had a pain in the leg made this model to ask the gods for a cure.

thought it was very important to provide medical services and a clean, hygienic environment.

Medicine for all

The Roman army had employed doctors for many centuries, and hospitals were provided in all military fortresses. Much of their work involved treating injured soldiers. Medical assistants called 'capsarii' bandaged wounds on the battle field. In the hospital it was the job of more skilled doctors to extract any weapons – arrows or spears, for example – left sticking in the wounds, and to stitch up cuts so that they would heal. Contemporary writers describe this kind of work. In more peaceful times, local people sometimes visited doctors in forts and fortresses to ask for advice. In this way Roman medical knowledge spread to the provinces.

In Rome itself, and in certain towns and cities of the Empire, free medical treatment was provided for the poor. Special doctors were paid by the government to take on this work, an arrangement which had also existed in ancient Greece. Rich citizens paid to consult a doctor – some of whom, like Xenophon, the Emperor Claudius' doctor in the first century AD, grew extremely wealthy as a result.

This scene from Trajan's Column shows Roman doctors looking after soldiers who were injured in battle.

From crumbs of bread and magic spells to science

'*To cure a person with bread stuck in the throat, place crumbs from the same loaf in each ear.*' This piece of medical advice was given by a Roman writer. As it suggests, many people were deeply superstitious. They looked for cures in magic, in herbal medicine – and in religion. You will see this by reading another Roman cure: '*For toothache, touch the tooth with the plant erigeron three times. Spit and replant the erigeron. The*

A patient receiving treatment for a wounded leg. In their work Roman doctors made use of a wide variety of skilfully made instruments – forceps, dilators, knives and other equipment.

tooth, so they say, will never ache again.' Many gods were believed to have power over health, like the Greek god, Asklepios, who became popular in Rome around 300 BC. Some sick people made a model of the part of the body which hurt them, and left it in a temple dedicated to Asklepios in the hope that this would produce a cure.

These attitudes gradually gave way to the more scientific spirit of the hospitals. Greek medical science was highly advanced, and many Greek doctors began to come to work in Rome. Greek ideas about medicine were important in training great scientific thinkers like Galen, who worked as a doctor in Rome in the second century AD.

THE COLONY

The colony was a special kind of settlement, a town set up by the Romans in territory they had conquered. The writer Suetonius tells us that in about 50 BC,

'The population of Rome fell as 80,000 men had been sent to colonies overseas.'

'The world is not big enough'

Rome grew from a small settlement on the River Tiber in about 800 BC, into a power which controlled the countries bordering the Mediterranean and others beyond. First the Latin people of Rome conquered the rest of Italy. Then their armies challenged other powers, like the empire of Carthage in North Africa. By about 100 BC, Rome controlled Sicily, Sardinia, Spain, North Africa, Macedonia, Asia Minor and Illyria (parts of modern-day Greece, Bulgaria, Yugoslavia and Turkey). These conquests were made while Rome was ruled as a republic. From about the time of Christ, Rome was ruled by emperors and more conquests were made, bringing Roman power further into Europe. Contemporaries were amazed by the extent of this mighty empire. Josephus, a Jewish writer in the first century AD, exclaims that *'the world is not big enough'* to hold the Romans. Many shared his opinion.

This coin was made by a powerful British tribe, the Catuvellauni people. When the Romans conquered Britain, they set up a colony at Colchester, in the territory of the Catuvellauni, and built a great temple where they worshipped the Emperor Claudius.

Ruling an empire

As Roman power spread, arrangements were made to rule the different areas conquered, and the Empire was divided up into units known as 'provinces'. The first

This portrait of two shop-keepers was painted in the Italian town of Pompeii. Thanks to the system of Roman roads, and to the peaceful conditions, artists and others found it easy to travel. This meant that styles of art and architecture spread from place to place.

province, Sicily, was set up before 200 BC. Many more were created. Under the Emperor Augustus, the provinces were divided into two groups. The emperor kept control of the most troubled areas where the army was required. These provinces were ruled by the emperor's representatives. More peaceful provinces were ruled differently.

Colonies were settlements of veterans (retired soldiers) who were given a plot of land to live on when they left the army. These settlements formed another important part of the way in which the Romans ruled the lands they conquered. The colony at Narbonne in Gaul (modern-day France) was among the first colonies established outside Italy. Others followed – they included Trier in Germany, Colchester in Britain and Timgad in Africa (modern-day Algeria). For the government in Rome, it was very useful to have centres of ex-soldiers on whose loyalty they could rely. By this method, the Roman way of life spread throughout the Empire.

'World-wide communications'

By building up an empire in many different lands, Rome brought together people of different racial backgrounds – Celts, Germans, Greeks and many others. Inscriptions can explain a great deal about how this happened. Here is the dedication cut on one gravestone set up in the north of England: *'To Regina, his freed woman and wife, this stone is set up by Barates of Palmyra. She was of the tribe of the Catuvellauni.'* This inscription tells us that Barates, a merchant from the city of Palmyra in the Arabian Desert, travelled to England, settled down there and married a woman from the Catuvellauni people, a tribe

from the south of the country. Barates' story was not at all unusual. Thanks to the excellent system of Roman roads, many people travelled from one part of the Empire to another, and mixed with those they met.

The words of one contemporary writer paint a striking picture of the way soldiers, officials, merchants and their families moved freely round Roman territory. He says, *'World-wide communications are set up within the Roman Empire, and living standards improve as goods are sent here and there.'*

This picture helps us to see how people travelled around the Roman Empire, sharing their ideas and way of life. It shows a temple that was built in Roman territory in Africa and was dedicated to Roman gods. The style of building shows how the Romans themselves developed ideas from the Greeks.

Roman peace

This writer praises Roman rule, and gives one very important reason for doing so: because the Romans enforced peace in the areas they conquered. The 'Pax Romana' (Roman peace) lasted for about 200 years from the time of Christ. After this, the Empire was attacked by Germanic tribes, and in AD 410 Rome was sacked by the Visigoths. Ruled from a new capital, Constantinople, the empire in the East survived. But in the lands of the Roman Empire in Western Europe, Roman peace – and the Roman way of life which the colonies had helped to develop – was at an end.

GLOSSARY

Aqueduct A water-course made in stone to bring water to towns and cities. Sometimes aqueducts ran high above the ground on a series of great arches; sometimes they ran underground. The word 'aqueduct' comes from the Latin language.

Archaeology A way of studying the past by looking at objects which survive from long ago: the remains of buildings, tools and other articles made by people of the time, the sites where they lived, and other remains. Archaeology is especially important in finding out about periods of history when written records were not kept.

Auxiliary A member of the Roman army who was not a Roman citizen. Many auxiliaries came from lands conquered by the Romans.

Barbarians A word used by the Romans for people who did not live in cities.

Centurion An officer in the Roman army.

Circus The stadium in which chariot races were held. These races were extremely popular with people throughout the Roman Empire.

Citizen A city-dweller with special rights and responsibilities. Citizens were expected to play a part in the way their city was run.

Colony A city established by the Romans as a place for retired soldiers to live and farm the land.

Empire Lands conquered and ruled by another city or country.

Forum (plural 'fora') A public square at the heart of many Roman cities.

Freed man/Freed woman A slave who had been set free.

Gladiator A fighter who was specially trained to take part in fights that were staged to entertain the public.

Hypocaust A system to provide heating for buildings like villas and baths. Hot air from a furnace was drawn into a cavity beneath the floors, and between the walls, heating the rooms above.

Inscription Words cut in stone or on coins. The word 'inscription' comes from Latin words which mean 'to write'.

Latifundia Large tracts of land in the Roman countryside. They were run as very profitable farms.

Mosaic A picture made out of small cubes of stone or glass. These cubes were known as 'tesserae'.

Pagans People who were not Christian in their religion, and worshipped gods like Jupiter, Juno and others.

Paterfamilias The man who ruled each Roman household. He had great powers over his wife, children, servants and slaves.

Peasant A poor person who lived in the countryside and farmed the land.

Peninsula A strip of land surrounded by the sea on three sides.

Province One of the areas into which the Romans divided the lands they conquered. Organizing their lands in this way helped them to rule very efficiently.

Shrine A small place set aside for religious worship.

Slave A man, woman or child who was not free, and had to work for the master or mistress to whom he or she belonged. Slaves had no rights in law.

Temple A building dedicated to the gods. Priests worshipped the gods here. The public were not usually admitted to the temples, which were normally closed; they opened only on special days.

Villa A country house belonging to a wealthy Roman. Many villas were fine and imposing buildings with rich decorations. Others were the headquarters of working farms, and were not quite as grand.

FURTHER READING

For Children

Marjorie and C.H.B. Quennell, *Everyday Life in Roman and Anglo-Saxon Times*, Batsford, 1959.

For Adults

J. Percival, *The Roman Villa*, Batsford, 1976.

A.L.F. Rivet, *Town and Country in Roman Britain*, Hutchinson University Library, 2nd edn, 1964.

N. Lewis, *Life in Roman Egypt*, Oxford, 1983.